Desert Elephants

Written by Hannah Reed

Flying Start
to Literacy®

Contents

Introduction

Desert elephants are elephants that live in the desert in one part of Africa.

These elephants know where to find food and water – even in the desert. No other group of elephants does this.

Chapter 1:

How are desert elephants different?

Desert elephants are different from other elephants.

They have bigger feet than other elephants. And their feet can spread out more than other elephants.

This stops them from sinking into the sand as they walk through the desert to find water.

Desert elephants can live on less water than other elephants. Most elephants must find water every day, but desert elephants only need to find water every three or four days.

Desert elephants often travel during the night, when it is cooler.

Chapter 2:
How do desert elephants find water?

Desert elephants use their senses to find water.

Desert elephants can smell rain. This helps them to find water.

Desert elephants have very good hearing. They can hear rain falling even when it is a long way away. This helps the elephants to get to the water before it soaks into the ground.

Desert elephants often travel along dry riverbeds. When there has been no rain for a long time, there is no water in the rivers and the riverbeds are dry.

But there is water under the dry riverbeds all year round. The elephants can smell the water when it is not far under the sandy riverbed.

They dig holes in the sand to get to the water.

Desert elephants can also remember when and where rain fell in the past. They travel to these places to wait for the rain to come.

Chapter 3:
What do desert elephants eat?

Desert elephants eat plants. They use their trunks to pick leaves, flowers and bark.

They also use their trunks to shake fruit and seeds out of trees.

Desert plants mostly grow near dry riverbeds. By following the dry riverbeds, desert elephants are able to find the food they need each day.

Desert elephants can remember where they found food before. They return to these places each year.

Desert elephants eat up to 300 kilograms of food a day, so they cannot stay in one place for very long. If they did stay in one place, they would quickly eat all of the plants that grow there.

Chapter 4:
How far do desert elephants travel?

Every year, desert elephants can travel more than 450 kilometres as they move from one water hole to the next. No other group of elephants does this.

As they travel, mother elephants teach their babies where to go and how to find food and water.

Conclusion

Desert elephants are amazing animals. They can live in the desert where most other large animals cannot live. They are very good at finding water and food in the hot, dry desert.

A note from the author

I did not know that desert elephants existed until I watched a television program about these amazing elephants. As I watched these huge animals walking through the desert, I was astounded at how they could find food and water in a place where I would surely not survive.

As I talked to my friends and family about these astonishing animals, I discovered that they didn't know about these elephants either. This made me eager to write a book about them so that everyone could learn about desert elephants.